TOM EDISON'S BRIGHT IDEAS

Copyright © 1989 American Teacher Publications
Published by Raintree Publishers Limited Partnership
All rights reserved. No part of this book may be reproduced or utilized in any form or
by any means, electronic or mechanical, including photocopying, recording, or by any
information storage and retrieval system without permission in writing. Inquiries
should be addressed to Raintree Publishers, 310 West Wisconsin Avenue,
Milwaukee, Wisconsin 53203

Library of Congress number: 89-3901

Library of Congress Cataloging in Publication Data

Keller, Jack, 1917-
    Tom Edison's bright ideas / Jack Keller; illustrated by Lane Yerkes

    (Real readers)
    Summary: A biography of the inventor, for beginning readers, focusing on his research
with electricity and his invention of the incandescent electrical light.

    1. Edison, Thomas A. (Thomas Alva), 1847-1931 — Juvenile literature.   2. Inventors —
United States — Biography — Juvenile literature.   [1. Edison, Thomas A. (Thomas Alva),
1847-1931.   2. Inventors.]   I. Yerkes, Lane, ill.   II. Title.   III. Series.
TK140.E3K425   1989   621.3-092 — dc20   [B]   [B2]   89-3901
ISBN: 0-8172-3532-9

        3   4   5   6   7   8   9   0   93   92   91   90

REAL READERS

TOM EDISON'S BRIGHT IDEAS

by Jack Keller
illustrated by Lane Yerkes

BRITANNICA BOOK CLUBS

Raintree Publishers
Milwaukee

Tom Edison was a boy who asked many questions. In 1852, when Tom was 5 years old, he asked, "Why does a goose sit on its eggs?"

His mother answered, "Birds sit on their eggs to keep them warm. The eggs must stay warm till it's time for the baby birds to come out of the eggs."

"Oh," said Tom. "I want to see the baby birds."

4

Tom did not just ask many questions.
He liked to see and try things, too!

The next day his father found Tom
sitting in a nest that Tom had made.
The nest was filled with goose eggs.

"I am keeping the eggs warm," said
Tom. "I want to see the baby birds come
out of the eggs."

Everyone thought that was funny!

When Tom was 8, he went to school for the first time. Tom wanted to learn. But the teacher said that Tom asked too many questions.

"I don't have time to answer Tom's questions," his teacher said. He had never met a boy like Tom before, and he did not know how to teach him.

Tom's mother said, "If the teacher at school can't work with Tom, I will teach my boy at home."

Mrs. Edison made learning fun for Tom, and he learned very fast. He liked reading, and he liked reading science books best of all. His reading helped him think up new ideas.

Tom had a notebook with him all the time. In the notebook he made pictures of the new things he was thinking about. He made pictures of machines that would help people do work.

"One day I will make these things," he said. "I will be an inventor."

Tom knew from the books he read that
scientists and inventors did experiments.
They would start with an idea and then
try it out to see if it worked. Tom
wanted to do experiments, too.

When Tom was about 10, he and his
mother made a lab in a room under the
house. Tom did his experiments there.

At first, Tom just did experiments that he read about in his books. But then he started to make up his own experiments, too.

One day, Tom was working in his lab and—BOOM!

"He will blow us all up some day!" his father shouted. Tom's experiment had made the house shake.

"Let Tom be," his mother said. She knew how much Tom loved his work.

When Tom was 12, he got a job. He wanted to help pay for his experiments. His job was to sell food and newspapers to people who rode the trains.

One day Tom was hurt on a train. After that, Tom did not hear well.

But Tom did not stop working and experimenting. "Time passes so fast," he said. "I have so many things to learn and do."

One thing he liked to read about and experiment with was electricity. He wanted to learn all about it.

Tom knew that lightning was a kind of electricity. "If electricity could make lights up in the sky," he thought, "maybe it could be used to make lights in people's homes, too."

People just smiled when Tom talked about lights that ran on electricity. At that time, people did not use electricity in their homes. They got light from candles and from lamps that used gas.

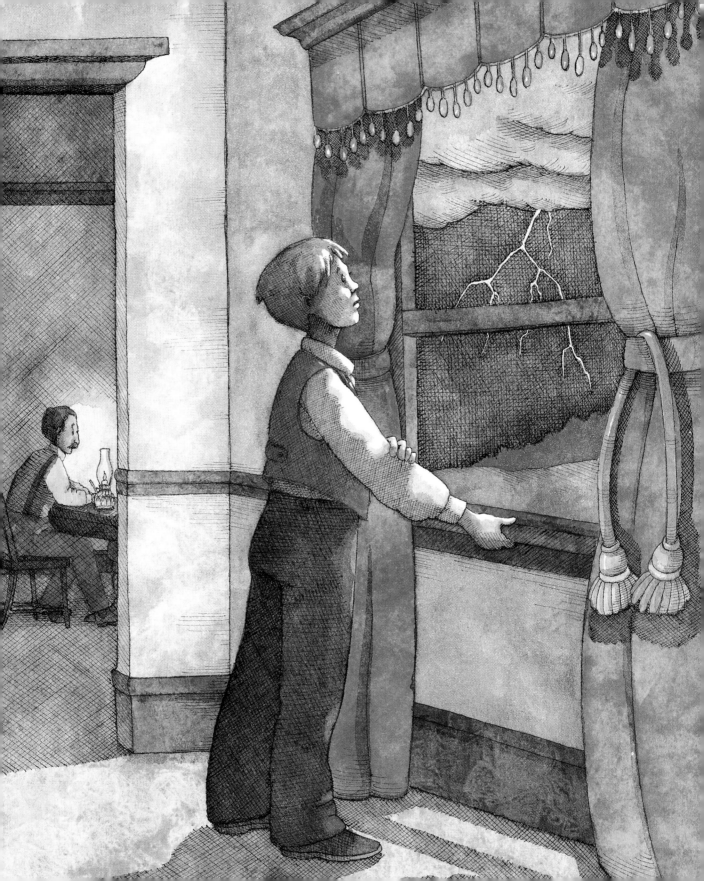

As a boy, Tom dreamed of the day when he would make new machines that used electricity. By 1868, Tom had begun to work on his dream. He was 21 years old and he was selling his inventions.

Tom did well as an inventor. He opened
a big lab in New Jersey. There he made
many of the inventions we still use
today. He did not invent the first
telephone, but he did make a new
telephone that was better. He did not
invent the first typewriter, but in 1871,
he did make a new and better typewriter.

He made many new machines of his
own, too. One was a machine that could
talk! It was the first record player.

In 1876, Tom was 29 years old. He now had a big new lab in Menlo Park, New Jersey. He had many people who helped him in his work.

People said that Tom was the best inventor that ever was. But Tom still had more ideas to try out. He still dreamed about inventing a light that ran on electricity.

Tom worked on his ideas for the new light. First, he made a glass bulb. He knew that if the bulb had just the right kind of wire inside of it, it would give off a bright light. The light would last a long time.

It took years, but Tom did not stop experimenting with wires. At last, in 1879, he did it! He found just the right kind of wire. People thought that the electric light was Tom's best invention yet!

In 1880, Tom started a factory to make electric light bulbs.

Soon after that, Tom worked on the idea of making a lot of electricity in a big plant. He wanted to send electricity to all the places where it could be used to do work.

He wanted electricity to be easy for people to use. He wanted it to be easy for people to make use of all of his inventions.

Tom Edison went on experimenting and inventing all of his life. He invented more than 1,000 things.

When people asked him, "How did you do all that?" Tom smiled and answered, "Anyone can do it. All you have to do is think!"

Sharing the Joy of Reading

Beginning readers enjoy reading books on their own. Reading a book is a worthwhile activity in and of itself for a young reader. However, a child's reading can be even more rewarding if it is shared. This sharing can enhance your child's appreciation — both of the book and of his or her own abilities.

Now that your child has read **Tom Edison's Bright Ideas**, you can help extend your child's reading experience by encouraging him or her to:

- Retell the story or key concepts presented in this story in his or her own words. The retelling can be oral or written.

- Create a picture of a favorite character, event, or concept from this book.

- Express his or her own ideas and feelings about the subject of this book and other things he or she might want to know about this subject.

Here is an activity that you can do together to help extend your child's appreciation of this book: You can conduct an electricity "treasure hunt" to help increase your child's awareness of the role electricity plays in our lives. Go from room to room of your home. In each room, ask your child to point out the things that run on electricity, while you keep a list. After the hunt, review the list together, and ask your child to suggest ways that you can conserve electricity (for example, turning off lights that are not in use, or not playing the TV if no one is in the room to watch it). Try to use your child's suggestions to conserve electricity together.